7-03

P9-DHT-617

T

HALLOWEEN FUN

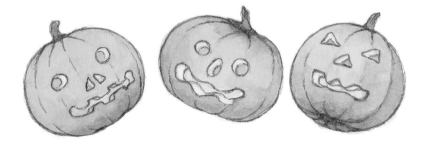

KINGFISHER

BOSTON

KINGFISHER
a Houghton Mifflin Company imprint
222 Berkeley Street
Boston, Massachusetts 02116
www.houghtonmifflinbooks.com

First published in 1993
2 4 6 8 10 9 7 5 3 1
1TR/0403/SF/FR/140MA

LIBRARY OF CONGRESS CATALOGING-IN-PUBLICATION DATA
Willis, Abigail.
Halloween fun/Abigail Willis, Annabel Spenceley.
—1st American ed.
p. cm.
Summary: Presents a collection of Halloween activities, including
making costumes, masks, cakes, spooky sounds, and shadows.
1. Halloween decorations—Juvenile literature. 2. Handicrafts—Juvenile literature.
3. Halloween cookery—Juvenile literature. [1. Halloween decorations. 2. Handicrafts.
3. Halloween cookery.]
I. Spenceley Annabel, ill. II. Title
TT900.H32W55 1993
745.594'1 dc20 93-21712 CIP AC

ISBN 0-7534-5683-4

Printed in China

CONTENTS

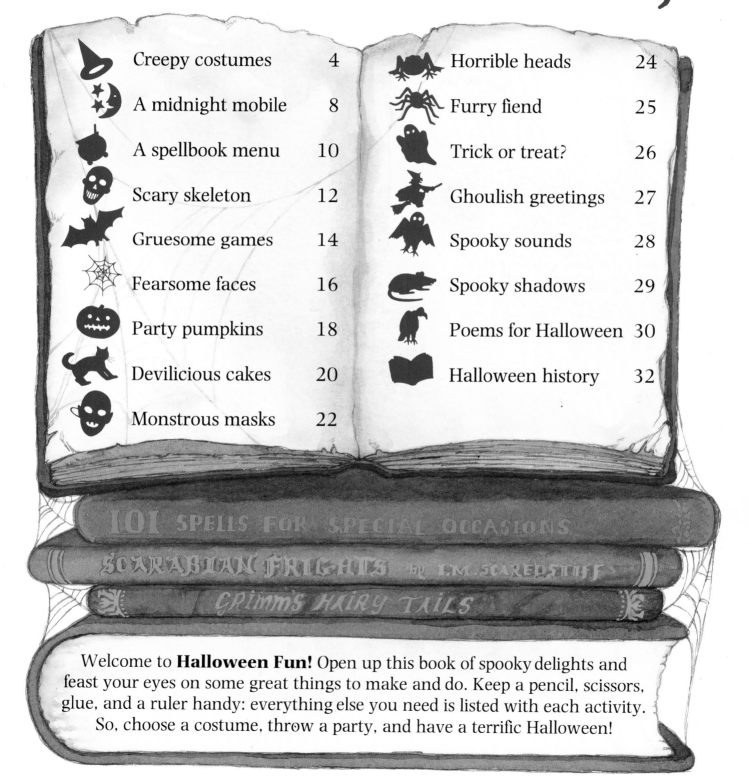

101 SPELLS FOR SPECIAL OCCASIONS

SCARABIAN FRIGHTS by I.M. SCAREDSTIFF

GRIMM'S HAIRY TAILS

Welcome to **Halloween Fun!** Open up this book of spooky delights and feast your eyes on some great things to make and do. Keep a pencil, scissors, glue, and a ruler handy: everything else you need is listed with each activity. So, choose a costume, throw a party, and have a terrific Halloween!

CREEPY COSTUMES

A good costume is essential at Halloween, and here are some great ideas for how to make your own. You could be a witch, complete with hat and broom, or maybe you'd like to be a spider — see over the page for the spookiest spider outfit you've ever seen. Also there are ideas on mummy, skeleton, and ghost costumes.

WITCH

You will need

Black fabric, needle and thread, green tinsel, stick-on stars, false nails, cardboard, black paint, a black garbage bag, a wooden pole, twigs, Velcro

2 Decorate the cloak with stick-on stars or glue on cut-out fabric shapes. Sew or glue the tinsel along the front edges of the cloak.

3 Glue on false nails, or paint your own nails a gruesome color.

Make your own magic broom simply by tying a bunch of twigs to a pole with string.

1 Make sure the black fabric is large enough to wrap around you. Sew or glue a 2-inch strip of Velcro tape on both sides of the cloak's neck so you can fasten it.

To make the witch's hat:

1 Cut a brim from the cardboard so the inside circle fits just over your head.

2 Roll another piece of cardboard into a cone shape. The base should fit over the inner circle of the brim.

3 Make small cuts in the brim and stick the tabs to the inside of the cone.

4 Cut a wide strip from a black garbage bag and cut slits along one side.

5 Tape the "hair" into the cone of the hat and trim bangs in front.

SPIDER

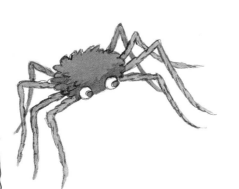

1 Take 3 pairs of black panty hose (the thicker the better) and cut them into 6 "legs."

2 Stuff the legs with plenty of scrunched-up newspaper and attach the top of each leg with a safety pin to a strip of strong black fabric long enough to be tied around your waist. Remember you only need to make 6 legs as your own make up 8!

3 Wear black leggings and a black sweater or leotard and decorate your top with a web design using white tape.

4 Glue 2 pipecleaners to a headband and attach 2 painted cardboard eyes.

◄ To make a slippery bat outfit, cut a black garbage bag along its seams to make it flat; cut along one edge to make bat-shaped wings, and attach to your arms with yarn threaded through the plastic and tied at the elbow.

▲ For a very simple but effective ghost costume, take a white sheet and drape it over you. Get a friend to mark with a pen where your eyes are, then take the sheet off and cut out eye holes. Put your sheet back on and get ready to spook!

► How about being a bony skeleton? You'll need to dress in black and then, using white tape or fabric paint, stick or paint on "bones" — just follow this picture. For a really effective look, paint your face like a skull — see page 37.

► To transform yourself into a mummy, wrap yourself in bandages (or bathroom tissue). Wrap your arms, legs, and body separately. Do not wrap anything around your neck or face. Color your face pale green or blue using face paints.

A MIDNIGHT MOBILE

When the midnight hour strikes, see the shapes of Halloween come to life. Make this simple mobile and hang it up every year — with a light October breeze, and the flickering light of a jack-o'-lantern, it's the perfect Halloween decoration.

You will need

Thin cardboard, tracing paper, a needle and thread, a wire coat hanger, paints

2 Paint one side of each shape using the pictures here as a guide. Paint the other side of your cardboard shape black.

1 Trace these shapes onto cardboard and cut out.

4 Finally, attach the other end of the thread to the coat hanger or to another shape, and watch your mobile take on a life of its own!

3 Using the needle, make a small hole at the top of each shape and pull the thread through, making a secure knot at one end.

A SPELLBOOK MENU

Halloween wouldn't be Halloween without some scrumptious, tasty morsels to eat straight from the witch's caldron. All these recipes are great for parties or even just for yourself! Ask an adult to help you when using a hot stove or sharp knives, and remember — a witch's hat (see page 5) should be worn at all times while you prepare your spellbook menu.

CRACKLE CACKLE CRUNCHIES

You will need

$2\frac{1}{2}$ cups breakfast cereal
8 oz. chocolate
2 tablespoons light corn syrup
Cupcake liners

1 Pour some water into a pan until it is about an inch deep and bring it to the boil.

2 Break the chocolate into pieces and put into a heatproof bowl. Put this into the pan until the chocolate has melted.

3 Stir the syrup into the melted chocolate and add the cereal.

4 Spoon into cupcake liners and leave to set.

WITCH'S BREW

You will need

3 pints purple grape juice
$1\frac{1}{2}$ pints club soda
Grapes and apples

1 Mix the grape juice and soda in a pitcher.

2 Halve the grapes and take out the seeds.

3 Cut the apple into small chunks.

4 Float the fruit in the brew just before serving: by magic, the grapes and apples will look just like eyes and teeth!

5 Make a swizzle broomstick from a straw and black paper cut into a fringe.

MONSTER SANDWICH

For a sandwich fit for a monster, use 3 or more slices of bread sandwiched together with your favorite fillings. Stack the slices up and carefully cut diagonally in half. Make a monster face on top of each half, using slices of boiled egg or cucumber for eyes, and a piece of ham, (or anything else you can think of) cut into a fanged shape for a mouth.

SLIME DESSERT

You will need

Cherry-flavored and lime-flavored gelatin
Whipped cream
M & Ms

1 Ask an adult to help you make equal quantities of cherry and lime gelatin.
2 When set, mash each color up separately.
3 Place alternate layers of slimy gelatin into a large glass bowl.
4 Top with "eyeballs" of whipped cream blobs with M & M centers.

CANDY APPLES

You will need

14 short wooden sticks
14 apples
1 lb brown sugar
3 oz. butter or margarine
2 teaspoons white vinegar
6 fl.oz. water
2 tablespoons
light corn syrup

1 Push a stick firmly into each apple.
2 Heat all the other ingredients in a pan until the sugar and butter have melted.
3 Bring to the boil for 5 minutes without stirring until a teaspoon of mixture dropped into cold water becomes hard. Then stand the pan in cold water.
4 Dip each apple into the mixture, then stand on a lightly buttered plate to set.

SCARY SKELETON

1 First trace all the shapes on the opposite page with a pencil and rub them down onto the cardboard.

You will need

White cardboard
Tracing paper
5 paper fasteners
A needle and thread

2 Cut each piece out and very carefully make the holes with the pointed end of a pair of scissors.

3 Attach the legs and arms to the body using the fasteners and link the two strips with the fifth fastener. Make sure that each part of the body can move easily.

4 Thread the needle with 8 inches of thread and use it to attach the head to the center of the strips. Knot both ends tightly. Using 10-inch lengths of thread, attach the hands to one of the strips and use 13-inch lengths to attach the feet to the other strip. Now just move the strips with your hand and your skeleton will leap into action!

GRUESOME GAMES

Halloween calls for out-of-the-ordinary games to play, so here are some unusual ideas. Invite some friends to join you, and prepare to jump out of your skin!

CRAZY CREATURES

You will need

A spiral-bound notebook
Felt-tip pens
A ruler

1 Draw two lines equally spaced across the first page of your notebook to divide it into three. Do this for at least eight pages, making sure that your lines are in the same place on each page.

2 Draw a different creature on each page, with the head at the top, the body in the middle, and the legs at the bottom.

3 Cut along the lines so you can turn each section on its own. Flip the pages back and forth and make crazy creatures by mixing up heads, bodies, and legs!

VAMPIRE CHASE

This game comes straight from your worst nightmare! You'll need some red stickers, and at least six people. Choose someone to be the vampire (to make them look really convincing, make them the mask on page 39 to wear); everyone else wears three red stickers. The vampire chases its victims around and, if someone is caught, the vampire takes a drop of blood (a red sticker). When someone loses all three stickers, they become the vampire—and so the game continues . . .

GHOSTLY GROANS

You'll need a large space for this ghoulish game and again, six people or more. Pick a "ghost hunter" and blindfold him or her. The other players or "ghosts" circle around the ghost hunter who must try to catch one of them. When someone is caught they must wail and moan in as ghostly a way as possible and the ghost hunter must guess who it is. If the ghost hunter guesses correctly he or she can change places with the ghost they caught. If not, the ghost goes free and the ghost hunter must try again.

FEARSOME FACES

To make a good costume look even better, try painting your face to match! Only use face paints — not the ordinary paint that you use for pictures. Use bold strokes, strong colors, and your imagination!

WITCH

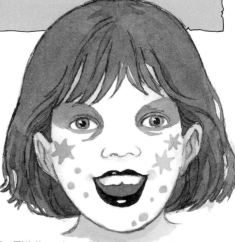

1 Use a white base color all over the face using a damp sponge.

2 Apply purple to the eyes, sweeping the color upward and outward.

3 Fill lips in with black and draw on stars and green warts.

SPIDERWEB

1 Apply white base color with a little pale green color blended around the edges.

2 Draw fine black lines around the eyes and from the nose to the edge of the face.

3 Join the lines with a spiral of black lines. Paint lips black and add a spider.

NIGHT AND DAY

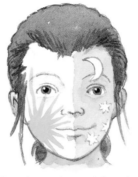

1 Paint one half of your face white and draw a sun and its rays in bright yellow.

2 On the other side, draw a moon above your eye and stars on your cheek in white.

3 Add pale blue clouds to your "daylight" side and color the "night" side dark blue.

For a vampire look, paint the face white with gray shadows around the eyes. Paint eyebrows black and make lips blood red, adding a few red drops on the chin. Finally, paint white fangs.

Frankenstein's monster is recreated using a green base on the face. Draw scars, outline the eyes in black, and paint the mouth blue.

To paint a skeleton face, use black and white face paints and copy the design below.

PARTY PUMPKINS

Without jack-o'-lanterns, Halloween just wouldn't be the same. Jack-o'-lanterns can look spooky or funny, depending on the way you cut your pumpkin. So, ask an adult to help you with the cutting, and follow this easy guide!

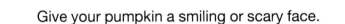

Give your pumpkin a smiling or scary face.

1 Get a big pumpkin and cut a circle around the stem. Make the hole big enough to fit your hand in. Scrape out the pumpkin pulp and seeds and save for later.

2 Draw on eyes, nose, and mouth with a pen and cut them out. Keep the face simple to make your lantern more effective.

3 Light a candle and burn a little wax to make a puddle inside the pumpkin. Hold a candle in the puddle until the wax hardens. Ask an adult to help you light it.

A HALLOWEEN FIGURE

All you need to make a spooky-looking scarecrow figure are some old clothes, newspaper, a pole or stick, and of course, a pumpkin. Simply stuff the clothes with scrunched-up newspaper and tie up the bottom of the legs and arms with string. Add gloves and shoes to make hands and feet and push the pole or stick into the neck of the figure. Cut a face into the pumpkin and push it onto the stick.

HALLOWEEN SNACK

To put every part of your pumpkin to good use, roast the seeds for a healthy snack. Preheat the oven to 350°F.

Rinse the seeds with water. Grease a cookie sheet with butter or margarine and spread the dry seeds evenly on it. Bake for 10–12 minutes until golden brown. Put on an oven glove, remove the pan, and allow to cool.

DEVILICIOUS CAKES

A witch's kitchen is never busier than at Halloween, and a really special party cake is fun to make and even better to eat! Ask an adult to help, and follow the recipe below for a delicious chocolate Witch's Cat Cake, or try making a cake in the shape of a bat or spiderweb...

You will need

A rectangular cake pan
13 × 9 × 2 inches
1 cup butter or margarine
1 cup superfine sugar
3 eggs
2 cups self-rising flour
2 tablespoons cocoa
4 mini jelly rolls
Licorice and green candy

For the Icing:
$1\frac{1}{2}$ cups confectioners' sugar
2 tablespoons cocoa
2 tablespoons hot water
$\frac{1}{4}$ cup butter or margarine
1 teaspoon vanilla extract
Chocolate sprinkles

1 Preheat oven to 350°F. Beat butter and sugar together in a mixing bowl until creamy. Add beaten egg gradually and then the cocoa (mixed with hot water). Sift the flour into the mixture until it is soft and light.

2 Line the pan with waxed paper and pour mixture evenly into it. Bake for about 30 minutes.

3 Allow your cake to cool on a wire rack. Then cut out a basic cat shape as shown. Use the spare cake to make wedge-shaped ears.

4 To make the icing, simply sift the confectioners' sugar and cocoa into a bowl, and gradually mix in the soft butter, water, and vanilla extract, until the icing is

creamy. Spread thickly onto the cat shape. Position the ears firmly and cover with icing. Shake a layer of chocolate sprinkles over as a finishing touch.

5 To make the cat's tail, stick the jelly rolls together and to the "body" with a little icing and cut the end of the "tail" at an angle to form a point. Cover the tail with icing.

6 Use licorice candy for whiskers and finally, green candy to make a pair of glowing eyes!

For the bat and spiderweb cakes use the same recipe. Make 2 round cakes, sandwich them together with chocolate icing, and cover with the same icing.

To make a bat, cut the round cake into a bat shape and decorate with licorice candy.

Create a spiderweb design, by making some white icing from confectioners' sugar and a little water. Dribble the white icing in a spiral shape then draw lines from the center outward using a toothpick. Add a toy spider!

MONSTROUS MASKS

You need the best possible mask to wear at a Halloween costume party. These pages show you how to make a frighteningly realistic papier-mâché werewolf mask, or if you don't have much time, how to make a simple Dracula cardboard mask. Either way, you'll look sensational!

You will need

A balloon, wallpaper paste, elastic, paints, yarn, newspaper

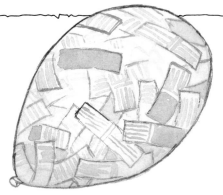

When you have made your basic mask, cut eye and mouth holes and use fresh papier-mâché to build a nose and ears. Then decorate your mask with paints and yarn.

1 Blow up a balloon roughly to your head size.

2 Next, mix wallpaper paste with water.

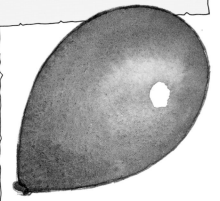

3 Cut up strips of newspaper and soak in the paste.

4 Cover the balloon evenly with layers of paper strips.

5 When the strips are dry, burst the balloon and cut the paper mold carefully in half with the help of an adult.

6 Make a hole on each side of the mask and thread with elastic.

Trace this mask onto thin cardboard and cut holes for the eyes and mouth. Paint on evil-looking colors and thread elastic through the holes.

HORRIBLE HEADS

Here's how to make some unusual
Halloween decorations . . .

1 Pierce both ends of each egg with a pin,
making one hole larger than the other.

2 Using the pin inside the egg, break the
yolk, then gently shake the egg, so the inside
becomes runny.

3 Blow into the egg's smaller hole over a
bowl so that the contents are forced out at
the other end through the bigger hole.

4 Rinse your eggshell with water, then use a
pair of scissors to make the bigger hole large
enough for your finger to fit into.

5 Now decorate your egg heads by
following the suggestions below.

Paint an evil face,
and glue on paper
shapes for Dracula.

Paint the
eggshell
green and
cover with
bandage strips
for a mummy.

You will need

Eggs, paints, a pin,
fabric, paper, yarn

Create a fierce
gorgon with
trailing hair
and painted face.

For a grinning
skull paint a bold
black pattern
on a white egg.

Use a piece of
white fabric
handkerchief
for a ghost
head.

FURRY FIEND

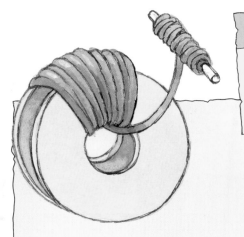

3 Tie a length of yarn
tightly around the middle.
Remove the rings.

1 Make a pompom by
winding some yarn
around 2 cardboard rings.

2 When the yarn almost
fills the center hole, ask
an adult to slide the blade
of a pair of scissors
through the yarn and
between the rings. Cut all
the way around.

4 Thread lengths of yarn
through the body with a
needle to make the legs.

5 Sew on beads to make
the eyes.

TRICK OR TREAT ?

Here's how to make the witch's candy house from *Hansel and Gretel* and your own bright trick or treat bag.

CANDY HOUSE

You will need

A shoebox
Strong cardboard
Colorful candy wrappers
Paints

Draw a plan like the one shown here onto a piece of cardboard. It should be as long as your shoebox lid (a) and twice as wide (b). Fold along the dotted lines to make a roof shape, and glue the edges to the top of the box.

Cut two squares slightly larger than the width of the box. Fold and cut these to fit the side of your roof. Stick in place. Now decorate your house.

CANDY BAG

Take an ordinary paper grocery bag and color a bold Halloween design onto it.

Cut strips of thin cardboard and tape them firmly to the top of the inside of the bag for handles.

GHOULISH GREETINGS

Whoever gets this card is in for a shocking surprise! The card fits flat into an envelope and pops up to frighten the wits out of the (un)lucky person who opens it.

You will need

Thin cardboard, felt-tip pens, medium-sized rubber band

1 Copy the design on the right onto the cardboard at the measurements given.

2 Color the witch's head and cut the card out. Cut the oblong hole in the middle of the card, making sure that it is slightly wider than the witch's head.

3 Fold the card along the dotted lines, folding away from you. Push the head through the hole as you fold.

4 Loop one end of the rubber band over the notches at the back, and the other end over the notches at the bottom. This is the tricky part — ask an adult to help if you find it difficult.

5 To put the card into the envelope, squeeze it lightly together so that the rubber band stretches and the card becomes flat. It will spring back into terrifying shape the moment the envelope is opened!

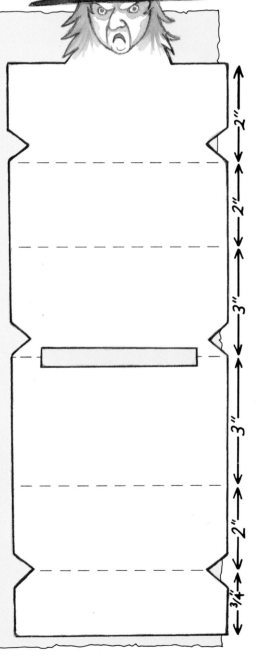

2"

2"

3"

3"

2"

3/4"

SPOOKY SOUNDS

Scary movies without spooky sounds wouldn't be scary at all — that's how important it is to create the right noises if you want to have a really eerie Halloween evening. If you have a tape recorder, try recording your own scary sound effects using the tricks shown here. Watch your friends' faces when you secretly play the tape back to them . . .

Rumbling Thunder

Take a large sheet of stiff cardboard. Holding it by the edges, shake it back and forth so that the middle part wobbles. This makes a rumbling thunder noise.

Hooting Owl

For a haunting owl hoot blow gently across the top of an empty bottle. To make higher or lower hoots, you can blow across bottles containing different levels of water.

Horses' Hooves

For the chilling sound of a phantom horse use 2 empty yogurt containers or plastic flowerpots. Tap them on a table to make a hollow clopping sound.

Creaks and Squeaks

Try opening a stiff door as slowly as you can for a haunted house sound effect. Or run your finger around the rim of a half-filled glass of water to make a strange, wailing noise. Shake a bag of dead leaves for a rustling effect. Often the best sounds are made with your own voice — try a cackling giggle or a deep-voiced laugh . . .

SPOOKY SHADOWS

For a flickering shadow show all you need is a bright lamp, a pale-colored wall, and your hands.

Here are some shapes to try, but you will soon find yourself inventing your own. If you have recorded any sound effects why not play your tape while you make your shadows?

Wait until it's dark, then shine the lamp on the wall and make shapes with your hands in front of the lamp's beam of light.

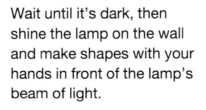

POEMS FOR HALLOWEEN

Nothing is scarier than a spooky tale read aloud on Halloween night. Here are some poems that will send shivers down your spine. Or, why not write some yourself with mysterious invisible ink. Just dip a pen with a nib into the cut half of a lemon and write your poem. To make the writing visible, hold the paper up against a warm radiator.

The Moon

The moon has a face like the clock in the hall;
She shines on thieves on the garden wall,
On streets and fields and harbor quays,
And birdies asleep in the forks of the trees.

The squalling cat and the squeaking mouse,
The howling dog by the door of the house,
The bat that lies in bed at noon,
All love to be out by the light of the moon.

ROBERT LOUIS STEVENSON

In the dark, dark wood, there was
a dark, dark house,
And in that dark, dark house, there was
a dark, dark room,
And in that dark, dark room, there was
a dark, dark cupboard,
And in that dark, dark cupboard, there was
a dark, dark shelf,
And on that dark, dark shelf, there was
a dark, dark, box,
And in that dark, dark box, there was
a GHOST!

ANON.

A skeleton once in Khartoum
Invited a ghost to his room.
They spent the whole night
In the eeriest fight
As to which should be frightened of whom.

Song of the Witches

Double, double toil and trouble;
Fire burn and caldron bubble.
Fillet of a fenny snake,
In the caldron boil and bake;
Eye of newt and toe of frog,
Wool of bat and tongue of dog,
Adder's fork and blindworm's sting,
Lizard's leg and howlet's wing,
For a charm of powerful trouble,
Like a hell-broth boil and bubble.

Double, double toil and trouble;
Fire burn and caldron bubble.
Cool it with a baboon's blood,
Then the charm is firm and good.

WILLIAM SHAKESPEARE

Witches fly skyward
Into the blackness,
Their passengers always
Cats of the darkest.
Halloween is with us,
Eve of All Saints, and
Spirits are stirring.

JOHN PATON

Queen Nefertiti

Spin a coin, spin a coin,
    All fall down;
Queen Nefertiti
    Stalks through the town.

Over the sidewalks
    Her feet go clack
Her legs are as tall
    As a chimney stack

Her fingers flicker
    Like snakes in the air,
The walls split open
    At her green-eyed stare;

Her voice is thin
    As the ghosts of bees;
She will crumble your bones,
    She will make your blood freeze.

Spin a coin, spin a coin,
    All fall down;
Queen Nefertiti
    Stalks through the town.

ANON.

HALLOWEEN HISTORY

The story of Halloween goes all the way back to ancient times. For the Celts who lived in Britain and Ireland at that time, New Year began on November 1. The night before, a festival was held to mark the change from summer to winter.

Because October 31 was the day the sun was at its lowest, it was believed that the sun entered the underworld for a short time, and, while the gates of the underworld were open, evil spirits were released to roam the Earth. To frighten these spirits away, the Celts lit huge bonfires, and dressed up as witches and ghosts.

In time, November 1 became a Christian festival day known as All Saints Day or All Hallows. The night before was called Eve of All Hallows and came to be called Halloween.

Early English settlers brought Halloween customs to the United States, but it was not until the 1800s, when many Irish and Scottish people arrived, that Halloween celebrations became really popular.

Today, most people don't believe in ghosts and witches, but it's fun to dress up as one for a costume party. The most important part of Halloween is to have as good a time as possible!